C000192580

Poetical Allsorts

with HARD &
soft centres

Poetical Allsorts

with HARD *&*
soft centres
By
Graeme Searle

Illustrated by
Dennis Bryans

First published in 2010

Printed and bound in Australia
by BPA Digital
11 Evans Street Burwood, Victoria 3125
for
Golden Point Press
P O Box 168
Blackburn South,
Victoria 3130

Designed and
Illustrated by
Dennis Bryans

Graeme Searle,
Poetical Allsorts
with hard and
soft centres
ISBN 978-0-9757673-9-9
1 Verse

CARPE DIEM

His bony fingers hold the pen and then
he thrusts the barbed end upon the page.
In rage — 'Methinks this work will never
   cease
until I die!'
But then the pen runs dry.

This book is dedicated to
my wife Helen, our children
and grandchildren.

CONTENTS

CLIFF

At Big River Cliff had made his camp
to work the fashion trade.
For it was he that trapped the rats
from which fur coats were made.

His house was just a one-roomed shack
of bark its walls and roof.
But snugly built by riverside
both warm and waterproof.

For door he'd hung a wheat bag
split down its length entire.
The lock he'd made from wooden peg
the hinges eight gauge wire.

1

Of Lysaght's corrugated iron
was the chimney at Hut's End
while polished stones comprised the
    hearth
brought up from River Bend.

Smoke blackened in the fireplace
above a red gum fire.
A camp oven and a billy hung
on hooks and chains of wire.

Of poles and Hessian was the bed
the mattress stuffed with hay.
A stripey pillow at its head
and blankets army grey.

A rough bush chair against the wall
a table made of deal
was where by light of Coleman lamp
Cliff sat and made his meal.

Cliff wrought by hand the traps he used
from golden syrup tins
by cutting cross in base of can
then pushing cut points in.

With fish he'd bait the clever snares
and ranging far and wide
he'd tie them all to snags and logs
down by the riverside.

The gentle long-tailed rodents
that scavenged on the shore
would poke their heads into the tins
but couldn't then withdraw.

Cliff walked along the trap-line
to collect the dead and dying.
Then stretched their pelts on wire
    frames
and hung them up for drying.

Now Cliff was just a simple man
his pleasures were but few.
At night he'd smoke an old bent pipe
or drink a port or two.

But then one day the buyer came
and with him brought some rum.
Cliff would have had a better day
if he had never come.

With rum all gone, the pelts were sent
to town with city sort.
And gaily Cliff tripped into hut
to celebrate with port.

Cliff sang and laughed beside the fire
until the port was drunk.
Then on his knees across the floor
he crawled into his bunk.

He lay two hours on his couch
until with thirst he woke.
Then opening up a gummy eye
he gave a little croak.

His brow felt like an anvil
by blacksmith being struck.
His tongue was thickly coated
with furry, sticky muck.

And when his unnatural thirst he'd
   quenched
he fell back on his bed.
And lay there quite unconscious
until the stars had fled.

The joyful carolling of magpies
beside the old hut's door
awoke Cliff on his bed of pain
and this is what he saw.

Cliff struggled into wakefulness
and raising up his head
looked unbelieving at his feet
splayed out at end of bed.

For stuck on end of Cliff's bare feet
alight in morning's glow
a glittering Golden Syrup tin
was gripping each big toe.

Cliff pried a lid from end of can
with horny nail of thumb
and saw inside a swollen toe
like a big black shiny plum.

The other foot was much the same
Cliff hobbled to the door
and walked on heels to neighbour's
    house
about three miles or more.

5

The kindly neighbour with his pliers
soon removed the jagged tin
and found a bucket full of turps
to soak Cliff's sore feet in.

With this generous sort of treatment
the toes healed up quite fast
though Cliff never drank of rum again
the time for that was past.

But if you're walking in the bush
along that lonely track
you'll hear Cliff rattling syrup tins
in his long gone ghostly shack.

BAROOGA STATE FOREST

In Barooga State Forest
by an anabranch flowing
we're camped on a beach
where the quinces are growing.

On a string from the clouds
and just out of reach,
the harvest moon hangs
like a giant Pullar's peach.

And the old dog went missing
but he's turned up with luck,
and he's now anchored firmly
to the back of the truck.

The boys and the girls
all head for the glade,
where they won't be disturbed
with their paper and spade.

But the caravan's packed
with our clobber and bedding,
and so to the highway
and home we are heading.

Yes, now we are leaving
the old river bend.
So goodbye to you all
and good evening friends!
(sung slightly off-key!)

KIDS!

The children don't wish
to partake of fish.
They say with a groan
there may be a bone!

GOOD INTENTIONS

Just when I think
I've got the drink mastered.
With the last cup
I finish up plastered.

URSUS HORRIBILIS

A bear stares out across the glade
from where the bush is thickest.
It's here the children's games are played
sweet kiddies playing cricket.

With amber orbs he eyes them all
then sees a tiny moppet
with cornflower eyes and bright red ball,
he sees the child soon drop it.

The child comes closer 'cross the grass
the bear lies on the ground.
The child's mouth ope's with startled gasp
oh bear! At last you're found.

Oh bear! I love you best of all
says child of only three.
And now she's lost her big red ball
but bear goes home to tea.

KOALA

Whilst gazing up in leafy gum
I saw aloft a furry bum.
A creature sat on padded haunches
resting there upon the branches.

Munching leaves for hours and hours
sniffing nectar-laden flowers
while safe within this mother's pouch
warm and snug on nippled couch

Lies a youngster pink and hairless
in that pocket nearly airless
for twenty weeks within this bower
as mother climbs the leafy tower.

When at last it shows its snout
blinks its eyes and comes out.
There's special food for this wee one
for it dines upon his mother's dung.

ANTECHINUS HOPPING MOUSE

Brown antechinus, hopping mouse
loves but once his pouched spouse.
For six long hours entwined they lie
then when they part through stress he'll die.

For near five weeks the young are found
on nipples fast and dragged around.
Beneath the mother as she munches
the arthropods on which she lunches.

Though mother's left to fend alone
she'll suckle young and find a home.
A grassy nest in stump or log
will keep them safe from cat or dog.

For a while, the young will hunt with Mum
she'll teach them all for she's a chum.
But come the winter cold and grey
the kids will leave and run away.

BOO-BOOK OWL

In the sheoak dark and old
lives an owl with eyes of gold.
A dappled feathered night time fowl
the boo-book or the spotted owl.

Upon a branch of flaking bark
was perched this creature of the dark.
Moon yellow was the orbed frown
he gave me as he turned around.

Just then I heard a tiny squeak
that came from out his curved beak.
And hanging down I saw, I think
a mouse's tail, soft haired and pink.

This little spotted owl so wise
then arched his brow and winked an eye.
And as he winked and gave a grin
he quietly sucked the rodent in.

EMU

Fletched with feathers wall to wall
the emu stands near six-foot tall.
The mighty thighed and feathered prancer
has drumsticks like a ballet dancer!
And at thirty knots across the plain
can pass a bike, though not a train.

The wondrous strong, athletic mother
has her eggs hatched by another.
Lots of 6 to 12 are found
like yolked avocadoes, on the ground.
The dear old cock without a fuss'll
hatch the eggs beneath his bustle.

For many weeks he'll take no food
and tend alone the lively brood.
Till he's quite thin
he can't be sane.
In two year's time
he'll try again!

HERON

White spectacled the heron
will wade through weed and sedge
to hunt the fish and froglets
that dwell at water's edge.

Its neck like bow by archer bent
will loose the stabbing arrow
of beak into the mirrored mere
to pierce the game below.

Then with its swollen crop it flies
to nestlings in their nest
in fork of giant river gum
to feed them, and to rest.

MAYFIELD 1948

My father had a Kelly axe
as sharp as sharp could be.
It stood beside the chopping block
beneath the old oak tree.

The chopping block beneath the oak
was used for poultry slaughter.
The axe that stood beside it
for making chickens shorter.

Out the boot of Dad's old chev
soon came our Xmas treat.
Two struggling bags of muscovy ducks
with lovely yellow feet.

Dad placed the bags beside the block
and selecting each discreetly
he hacked their heads off one by one
and did it very neatly.

Like a bunch of politicians then
they formed a chorus line.
Six headless ducks a dancing
beneath Mum's washing line!

RATS

We had a great big feed bin,
To keep the chook food in.
It was alive with baby rats,
So we chucked the old cat in.

No sooner was he in the bin,
Then he was out again.
He fled out of the old barn door,
With rats attached to him.

Next went in old Pete the dog,
The action it was hot.
He wouldn't leave that feed bin,
Until he'd killed the lot.

Looking back some sixty years,
It still feels like good fun.
When our dog was in the feed bin
And the rats were on the run!

SNAKE

Beneath the floorboards of the shed
there lives a giant copperhead.
Sometimes it comes into the house
in search of rat or little mouse.

It races through the walls and ceiling
a thing I find quite unappealing.
I really wish that rotten snake
would chase the frogs beside the lake.

IF I HAD THE WINGS OF A BEE

If I had the wings of a bee
I'd fly to the nearest gum tree.
And kiss its fringed flowers
for hours and hours.

And think, oh my darling, of thee!

CLEVER CHOOK

I used to have a clever chook
she was smart, could read a book.
She pecked each sentence with her beak
and for the rude words used to seek.
But when she swore I drew the line
and roasted her - she tasted fine!

HOME MADE

Our chook house was the very best
Of kero tins were made each nest.
Its hardwood frame could not be beat
With clouted on asbestos sheet
And chicken wire galvanised
Kept the chooks all safe inside.
Of Rhode Island Reds we had a few,
Black Orphingtons, and Leghorns too.
And every day on little legs
We helped our mum collect the eggs.

MYSTERY OF THE VANISHING SOCKS

In the laundry stands infernal
white machine that gleams external.
And with bumps and grinds internal
cleans the clothes for us eternal.

We set its little dials and clocks
to wash our shirts and clean our jocks.
As spinning round it weaves and rocks
and tears the clothes and eats the socks!

MARK'S BIG TOE

With bladder bursting
one dark night
my brother rose to pee.

His feet moved fast
across the floor
a chair he failed to see.

He hurried fast
and faster still
across the polished parquet.

Till chair leg met
and broke the toe
of elder brother Markey!

EATING YABBIES WITH KATE

We've got a copper on our farm
beneath a tree beside the barn.
We fill 'er up with clean tank water
me and Kate the youngest daughter.

We split the wood and light the thing
and then we chuck the yabbies in
and when they're boiled and go bright red
we eat them all on buttered bread.

THE CON MAN

Hullo! I knew your father
And went to the school on the hill.
I have never ever been bad
and you can call me Bill.

For years I was a magistrate
honest and gun-barrel true.
So if you've an egg in your basket
I'll double your money for you.

Did you know that I'd worked for Winston?
I also worked as a spy.
I'm a very important churchwarden
who's never been known to lie.

People come and people go
it's easy to advise them.
I bring them in and sit them down
and quickly hypnotise them.

Investment-wise they come to me
it's my advice they seek.
The money keeps on rolling in
at three-per-cent a week.

Sadly though I've blown the cash
still I'm not inclined to worry.
It serves them right to come to me
in such a tearing hurry.

For thirty years I've bled you dry
and now the cash is spent.
Don't ask me how, for I don't know
just where that money went!

MONTY

My daughter had a cat called Monty,
How she loved that pussycat.
While in the garden was a snake,
Eight feet long and fat.

One day the cat became the lunch,
Of the carpet snake a-writhing.
For old times sake she kept the snake,
And called it, Monty's python!

MOTH'S DAY

An egg hatched on a cherry tree
and then two more, so there were three.
The caterpillars thusly born
left the egg shells they had torn.

And to the store on eighteen feet
they trooped to buy their mum a treat.
For it was Moth's Day for the three -
and moth, she lived up cherry tree.

They bought a flower gift for Mum
a giant white chrysanthemum.
Then while they climbed the tree of green
the flower changed to clotted cream.

So, plucking cherries by the score,
they knocked upon their old Moth's door.
And Moth's Day dinner was a good'un
with cream and cherries for the puddin!

GOANNA

In the warm sunny weather
with a skin like worn leather
a lizard stretched out in the sun.
As was his habit
he dined off young rabbit
and now sniffed the air with his tongue.

Though he'd had a small feed
he still felt the need
of something more tasty to eat.
He hadn't missed out
but he lifted his snout
and rapidly got to his feet.

He walked past the dam
with its carcass of ram,
but it now was but leather and bone.
Till at last on the track
he neared the bark shack
of an old fella who lived quite alone.

So now with his nose bent
he followed a scent

past the privy and on down the track.
With all senses alert
he saw a red shirt
on the man on the porch of the shack.

With but one desire he climbed up the wire
of the chook pen and fell down quite hard
and the chooks started leaping
while the lizard was streaking
through the feathers and dust of the yard.

His face was directed
to eggs unprotected
their contents he spread far and wide
and he made a great din
as he ravaged each tin
with their eggs laid so carefully inside.

Now in the midst of the fun,
came the man with a gun
and his eyes they gleamed cold and hard.
But his old gun of rust
when he fired it bust
and he killed every chook in the yard.

The goanna ran out
with two yolks in his mouth
and headed at once for the hills.
The man dropped his gun
in the old chicken run,
then walked back inside feeling ill.

And the lizard we find
where at last he had climbed
to the top of an old wooden rail
then looking around
he suddenly found
he'd lost half a foot of his tail.

So we'll leave the man there
in his hut on a chair
with a pile of dead leghorns beside him.
For he'd really no luck
for they're all there to pluck
and he hasn't a chicken surviving!

TELL ME PLEASE!

To: Director Entomological Department
Arthur Rylah Institute.

Dear Sir or Madam tell me please
what are these creatures in my trees?

On Sunday morning when I stood
beneath a pine tree splitting wood.
I saw sitting on my barrow
a giant five-inch caterpillar.

Lined, zebra-like in white and black
he was stripped down side and back.
Golden medals down each side
he was wearing with silent pride.

And on each flank were hairy tufts
some of white and some of rust.
And at the rear were eight strong grippers
upon which he wore soft yellow slippers.

His red-whiskered face he turned to me
then he smiled, and ambled up the tree.

BLUEY'S FRIEND

Black watered lies the billabong
Beneath the ghostly gums
And ghastly rise the rotting eyes
Of bubbles in the sun.

The opal fingered mists of dawn
Through sweating tussocks creep
Its tendrils pass the portals dark
Where viper lies asleep.

Beneath an ancient river gum
On bank of Oxbow lake
There lies a long-dead mother's son
Who died by tiger snake.

The native bees have made a home
In what was once his chest
And in his softly curling beard
A blue wren has made its nest.

And Bluey lies beside him
A hand lies on his head
For he never left his master
Now he too lies long dead.

THE SEARLE

(In deference to 'Banjo')
Alan H.

I have just received your letter
And now feel so much better
Having been invited
To attend your birthday bash.

'Mongst all your mates that matter
We'll gather for a chatter
And drink your health sincerely
In the old traditional way.

I'll surely be delighted
In fact I'm quite excited
To be there at Jimmy Watson's
Where we'll celebrate the day.

In recent times I've been pensive
And even times defensive
Of the state of our existence
On this our planet earth.

But I've thought it out completely
And it comes out quite neatly
Having friends like you mate
Make it all so worthwhile!

FAIRIES IN MY GARDEN

There are fairies in my garden
Beneath the apricot
There's Gnomes and Trolls and
    Leprechauns
We've got the bloody lot

And down behind the barbeque
In the heat-bead bin
There lives a little Goblin
With wings as black as sin

And in the hours of darkness
He sits upon a stump
A-plucking wings from Elves and things
The rotten little ****

NED

Blue the copper found young Ned,
Two black ducks by his side.
'I've got you now, you reprobate
You're gunna go inside.'

'How did you get them ducks?'
The local sergeant said.
'Well one of them attacked me
It flew right at me head.'

'If that's the situation,'
Said old Sergeant Blue.
'You should have only shot the one
That was the sporting thing to do.'

Ned said, 'They're very hard to tell apart
I mean it's hardly fair.
I didn't know which one it was
So I had to shoot the pair.'

That night down at the station,
There was roast duck on the table.
It's always wise to compromise,
With coppers when you're able!

GINGE

Mum brought a ginger kitten home,
I've no idea where from.
And it wasn't long before the cat became
A great big ginger tom.

'The time has come at last,' said Dad,
'To look at his essentials.'
So turning Ginger upside-down
He checked on his credentials.

'Grab that gumboot son,' he said,
We'll stick him into that.
Ginge seemed a little apprehensive
For he was a well hung cat.

The cat was in the gumboot,
His tail up in the air.
Dad brandished Mum's new scissors
To remove the offending pair.

The scissors quickly did the job,
Two snips was all it needed.
The cat was eager to reverse
And very near succeeded.

We let old Ginge out of the boot,
The cat he didn't linger.
That was the day Dad cut the cat
And nearly cut his finger!

THE CAT BOX

Like a cat in comfy sandbox
Old Splinter hunkered down.
He squatted beside a warren
and he quietly looked around.

But oh! what a stroke of misfortune
for his knackers he suddenly found.
In the jaws of a rusty old rabbit trap
and he leapt to his feet with a bound.

But alas, he didn't quite make it
and oh! how exquisite the pain.
For he'd only moved twelve inches
when he finally ran out of chain.

NED

Ned kept a goat down in the shed
To keep him company.
For in the shed it was that Ned
performed his dentistry.

Whenever Ned had toothache
He'd walk down to that shed.
To return a little later
With a tooth less in his head.

In the shed, upon the bench
He kept his pliers handy.
And in the goat's bed he had hid
A pint of good French brandy.

He'd totter back into the house
A smelling of strong drink.
And spitting bits of gum and bone
Into the kitchen sink.

Till finally he had but one
The last offending tooth.
But his pliers couldn't do the job
That canine stood aloof.

So Ned went to the dentist
Who was to the manner born.
The job was very quickly done
That yellowed fang was drawn.

The dentist said, 'We'll take a wax
   impression.
Of your mouth for dentures new.'
Ned replied, 'I have a brother in the game
I'll want no teeth from you!'

'Oh!' said the dentist, 'does he work
For Nankervis, the premium false teeth
   maker?'
'No', said Ned, 'he works for Dyson
The local undertaker!'

The late Mayor's daughter married Ned
'Twas not his wealth but rather
Something about his toothy grin
That reminded her of her father!

FRUIT CAKE

My mother said to me, 'Now Joe
This year we are going to the Royal Show
and when we go we will take
what I have baked – a lovely cake.

With fruit and eggs I have been handy
I also added Granma's brandy.
I've mixed and kneaded with much lovin'
and popped it in the old camp oven.'

So, together with some luck,
we fired up the old Chevvy truck
and headed to the Melbourne Show.

When we arrived, the cake we took
in to the pavilion hall of cooking.
We left the cake there for the judging
and round the showgrounds we went
    trudging.

When at last the day was done
we headed back to see who'd won.
And it was with some surprise
to see that Ma had won a prize.

Thrilled she was with eyes lit up,
to see that she had won a golden cup.
A cup perpetual with blue ribbon
Was the prize that she was given.
Its bold engraving caught my eye
Highest count E Collii

BLOWIE

Mother blowie did her job
when on a sausage she did lob.
And very soon it could be shown
the poor old banger was well blown.

Sown with maggots down its stalk
with legs enough to make it walk.
Ma says it will have to go
into the fridge for old Fido.

Then Pa comes in, fresh from the bar
and opens fridge to choose a jar.
Then, looking round says to Mother
That sausage was good – is there
    another?

THE ONE TREE PUB

Out in the yard of the One Tree Pub
beneath moon's brilliant light
a festering mound of rotting rags
lay snoring in the night.

Old Splinter moaned and dreamt a dream
of drought on searing plain
and, as he dreamt, he seemed to scent
the smell of coming rain.

Then, from on high fat steaming drops
upon his head rained down
and dropped upon his gabby face
to dribble on the ground.

The welcome moisture from above
soon soaked his gritty beard
and coursed the seams on filthy face
and whiskey sodden head.

With trembling hands he seized his hat
as from the dream he broke
and tongue clove fast to roof of mouth
until at last he spoke.

'Oh Hughie,' cried out Splinter.
'You've sent the rain at last
I'll go and tell the publican
The drought, thank God, is past.'

So, swaying in the moonlight,
and though the lamp-lit door
he threw his hat into the air
and capered round the floor.

On high he held the sodden felt
for one and all to see
and 'Men' he quoth 'the drought just broke
as I lay beneath that tree.'

The barman peered at Splinter's eye
all bleary from his jag
and pulling makins from his strides
quietly rolled a fag.

'Now Splinter, settle down,' he said
and blew a ring of smoke.
'From what I say you'll get a laugh
for you can take a joke.'

'I saw you resting in the yard
beneath the old gum tree
and watched the yellow dog go past
then pause beside your knee.

'Now Splinter, here at One Tree
if you're drunk on Angus Brut
don't sleep it off out in the yard
best flake out in your ute.

'For if you sink beneath that tree
and are from grog half dead
the local dogs are sure to pass
and piss all down your head!'

13th SEPTEMBER 1990

I don't like old Laurie at all
For I like to hunt duck in the fall

But whatever the reason
If there were a season

I'd have his head up on the wall

HERBIE WOOD

Old Herbie was a full-blood
he used to poison stumps.
But Herbie has no fingers now
just thumbs and little bumps.

Old Herbie used to bore the holes
then stuff the poison in.
And always used a finger
to scrape it from the tin.

Old Herbie poked the arsenic in
with fingers from the pot.
The poison made him fingerless
now thumbs is all he's got.

Old Herbie cannot roll a smoke
it's hard to wipe his bum.
For now his digits are all gone
he's only got two thumbs.

But though old Herbie's fingerless
he'll shake nubs when he meetcha.
He likes his hands just as they are
they really are much neater.

EUCALYPTUS FREE

There is an awful euchy smell
in every park and garden.
To rid us from this stink, then, well,
our hearts we must enharden.

Let's clear the land of every tree
with billhook and with axe.
Until we're eucalyptus free
and can at last relax.

TAWNY FROGMOUTH

The tawny frogmouth marbled grey
looks like a stump when seen by day.
So when you're striding through the bush
give every stump a gentle push.

Push softly now and don't be cruel
one doesn't want to be a fool.
As through the bush with club we lurch
to flush each feathered stump from perch.

MISTAKEN IDENTITY

I tied up my old trailer
With strong green nylon twine
To hold within its iron cage
A load of junk and grime
And towed it to the crib point tip
Behind my red Toyota
Where gateman stood with gum
In mouth and made me pay my quota.

I cast my eyes around the joint
This dirty, boggy dump.
And watched a bird that flew across
And landed upon a stump
I said, 'My man what bird is that?
So big and black and showy?'
He answered, 'Mate, that's not a bird
It's just a crib point blowy!'

SPLINTER'S TEA

Splinter rested on a rail
his withered arms and long.
And proudly spoke about his tea
thick with bite, and strong.

'For years' he said, 'I drinks me tea
over campfire brewed and black.
Unless of course I was at home,
then I brewed it in me shack.

I'd drink Earl Grey and Bushells
Orange Pekoe and Soo Chong.
But never found a brand I liked
though I searched both hard and long.

I never found a brand,' he said
'that really suited me.
But an answer lay quite close at hand
an additive to the tea.

My tea was weak for years and years'
said Splinter looking wistful.
'But now I have the answer here —
bullants by the fistful!'

PUD

Pud potted rabbits near all night
and as he felt quite jaded
he went and fetched a chilly can
from where the grog lay shaded.

And fifty pair o'bunnies lay
in back of Holden Ute.
He hadn't missed a mark all night
though drunk as any newt.

He spilled the corpses on the ground
and grabbed his rabbit set.
Then sat upon a cartridge box
to give his feet a rest.

Now taking off both boots and socks
he felt the blessed breeze
that blew across the yellow dam
to cool his feet and knees.

Then as he shaved the hair that grew
and curled upon his calf
to test the edge of shining knife
he thought, My gawd that's sharp!

Then while he gutted bunnies
and watched the spreading dawn
a bullant climbed upon his foot
and nibbled at a corn.

The big ant's movement caught his eye
as it wandered to and fro
and swiping fast with razor steel
he severed his big toe.

The bullant stung him on the foot
and went upon its way.
While Pud danced round upon one leg
it really spoilt his day.

Now if you are a hunter
don't be a silly coot
and wave your knife at bullants
unless you're wearing boots.

For in the blood-red sand hills
there rusts a Holden Ute
with at its wheel a bloodless corpse
that isn't wearing boots.

NO SPARROWS IN W.A.

A poem to a friend in the West

Herewith, enclosed a clutch of eggs
to hatch between your cheeks.
And please, old boy, don't cross your legs
for a fortnight or three weeks.

These freckled orbs I gained for you
from nest in peppercorn.
And put in stove – about mark 2
to keep them safe and warm.

Now when at last in feathers brown
they're fledged and wish to fly
release them in a country town
by silos wheat or rye.

Then on their wings your name will rest
from York across to Barrow.
For you have brought in now from the east
the rotten bloody sparrow.

CLAUDE THE SAUSAGE

A dear old sausage called Claude
was really exceedingly bored.
This feeling he found delightful
for being eaten was frightful!

BANGER

Of sausage many times I ate
a banger was a dear old mate.
Until one day I found too late
half a maggot on the plate!

CLANCY'S SPARE PARTS SHOP

If you feel you're going blind
It's time to speak to Clancy
For blue or brown I know he'll find
An eye to suit your fancy.

BIGGLES

I can put up with the magpies
I can put up with the crows.
I can put up with the rooster
Which in the morning crows.

But the bark of little Biggles
is a strain too much to bear.
My head is getting thin on top
for I'm pulling out my hair.

The noise begins before the dawn
at six or five or earlier.
I'd knock upon the owner's door
if I were just a little burlier.

The neighbours yell at Biggles
there's a chorus in the dark.
That must be heard from Box Hill north
right down to Wattle Park.

So Ranger, please, put on your mask
and mount your steed of white
with Tonto do what must be done
to make that dog go quiet.

Now though the sound of gunfire
might be a bit too much.
You could use a hand-tooled riding boot
to kick him up the crutch!

YOUNG BUSINESS MEN

Businessmen squash fit, alert,
in flowered or striped business shirt.
In Clichy are both wined and dined
stop now chaps or you'll go blind!

THE WAX FLEA

The wax flea
   makes its lair
        in the hair
              of old men's ears.
              It leers
        at passers-by
   like bumblebees
and the common fly.

DOWN TO EARTH

This morning as I lay abed
I felt the stir of budding wings
and leaping from the sagging couch
I soared aloft upon the wind.

Then rising through the autumn air
ascending sunbeams as a stair
I flew beyond the city drear
into the bushland sweet and clear.

And as I flew in the clear blue sky
I thought I was a fairy,
but when I looked I found that I
was a blowfly black and hairy!